TENDERFOOT

Chris Beckett was born in London but grew up in Ethiopia in the 1960s. His first Carcanet collection, *Ethiopia Boy* (Carcanet/Oxford Poets, 2013), was described by Julian Stannard in Poetry Review as 'a series of dazzling vignettes... a love letter to the country and his childhood friend, Abebe'. His translations of contemporary Ethiopian poets have appeared in *Modern Poetry in Translation*, *PN Review*, *The Missing Slate* and *Asymptote Journal*. With Alemu Tebeje, he translated and edited *Songs We Learn from Trees*, the first ever anthology of Ethiopian Amharic poetry in English, published by Carcanet in May 2020. *Sketches from the Poem Road (after Matsuo Bashō's The Narrow Road to the Deep North)*, a collaboration with his partner, the Japanese painter and sculptor Isao Miura, was published by Hagi Press in 2015 and shortlisted for the Ted Hughes Award. He is a trustee of the Anglo-Ethiopian Society and the Poetry Society.

Also by Chris Beckett, from Carcanet

POETRY

Ethiopia Boy

AS EDITOR

Songs We Learn from Trees: An anthology of Ethiopian Amharic poetry

CHRIS BECKETT

Tenderfoot

CARCANET

First published in Great Britain in 2020 by
Carcanet
Alliance House, 30 Cross Street
Manchester M2 7AQ
www.carcanet.co.uk

A CIP catalogue record for this book is
available from the British Library.
ISBN 978 1 78410 971 4

Book design by Andrew Latimer
Printed in Great Britain by SRP Ltd, Exeter, Devon

The publisher acknowledges financial
assistance from Arts Council England.

CONTENTS

HERE COMES A DONKEY, LOADED WITH HOPE

for Isao

Tenderfoot: *a newcomer or novice, especially a person unaccustomed to hardship* (OED)

For now I ask no more than the justice of eating!
Pablo Neruda, *The Great Tablecloth*

I have already enjoyed too much, give me something to desire.
Samuel Johnson, *The History of Rasselas, Prince of Abissinia*

INGLIZAWI NEGN!

Sometimes he stands on the balcony in his blue pyjamas
and sees it through the eucalyptus trees

slips out when day is lapping at the dark
and stands there looking over garden gates and walls

over tin roofs clicking in their shadows
down a track that wanders into the evening

out towards the faintly green distance of hills
already stirring with bats and the idea of pumas

he can hear bells and bits of conversation   someone far away
banging a nail   knows himself to be small and foreign

standing on the balcony of a big quiet house
that holds him up   holding him like a hand under his feet

but never feels unwelcome in the semi-dark
if someone hails him from the track he will call back *Selam!*

if someone asks   *where are you from, little boy?*
he will answer proudly   *Inglizawi negn!*

he does not really know right now where English is or what
but is not troubled by the things he does not understand

while his eyes follow silhouettes of long-tailed birds
and he feels this moment stretch almost forever

አህያ መጣች ፥ ተጭና ባቄላ
aheya met'ach, tech'na baq'ela

here comes a donkey
loaded with beans

SWEETHEART

Yemisrach puts an arm
   around her husband
whispers *hodé!* in his ear

because here you say
   my stomach
not *my sweetheart*

and I say   how on the nose
   that stomachs stand
for love   here in Ethiopia

where people still admit
   how close a crop
and with it every

masticating
   sugar-burning
striding, strumming

circuitry of science
   art, philosophy
can come to being lost...

Yemisrach wets our hands
   and towels them
then Gedilu loads up

a pouch of injera
  one-handed
with a zilbo stew

hodé! he says
  as he says every day
the first mouthful is for you

GOOD BREAD

for Abebe i.m.

Still warm and spongy   almost wet
a circle of injera on the mesob
sits in my mind's eye and goes with me
reaching its gentle hand into my head

it makes me think about the day
your father took us to a market
in the hills   that red-eyed roadside boy
furiously begging to be fed...

do any of us really understand, Abebe
how finger close a boy can be
and still have nothing   nothing
of the world's good bread?

ASFAW'S HUNGER

It was the smell of onions frying
coaxed his question out...

what rumbles in your tummy, Asfaw?

Hunger! Asfaw booms

boy plants an ear

I hear a donkey and two taxis tooting!

But is the donkey happy?

there are buses grinding   scooters shrilling
drovers thwacking   hawkers hooting
a priest with shoes but no shoelaces (hear it!)
cursing every idle beast with hellfire, snakes etc

and   loud and clear

two grunting sacks of beans   one unruffled donkey
flop-eared   fly-tailed   calm as granite
in the middle of the mayhem highway   munching
its crisp hay

fuck off, old priest!

the donkey brays
and keeps on munching

Asfaw, your hunger stands its ground!

RAS GUGSA'S KINDNESS

The man who wrote this poem:

A man who loses his faith
will be buried in a field
and the earth will not cover his feet

who built churches and endowed them
gathered scholars of the Four Books
scholars of the great hymns of Yared
and many scholars of the different hymns

who prepared banquets for all his scholars
on the days of Christmas, Easter
and Epiphany, Annunciation
Ascension and Transfiguration

who ruled Begemder twice   from Beshelo
to Metemma   from Bambelo on the edge
of Wegera   following the basin of Lake Tana
even into the high Simiens

who was loyal to friends but great enough
to rebel whenever he felt like it
who had tents put up on Ajebar Field
so that his scholars could lie down

completely drunk on buckets of his t'ella
and flasks of his thick golden t'ej
after they had eaten all his white injera
and his everyday injera

trapping the thick sauces and tender meats
in strips of his delicious injeras
discussing the great hymns of Yared
while their lips and fingers became sticky

a man who died in battle
who when he died, three famous scholars
died with him   a man who even
in the worst confusion of the battlefield

until 11 o'clock in the morning
when he was killed
was seen handing out trays of food
and his friends, even his enemies, exclaimed

Ras Gugsa welcomes his own death with kindness!

THE TABLE

Even if a house is only mud and straw
a light bulb flickering by its blue tin door

even if a father shouts at one of his sons
and his other children smirk being the goody ones

even if a sweet girl hands out dishes of pea flour
and creamed spinach over the ridge of shoulders

until the table if it could talk would probably
say stop! and this is the moment most wobbly

when the mother hurries in with a giant pan
of fried beef t'ibs she ladles onto the injera…

even so, all anyone remembers now
is the way their mother wailed and how

she never stopped   meal after meal   as if
she was sleep-walking as she did it

and the little house shook with her unhappiness…
years later, resting on a sofa in her Sunday dress

her children now grown up ask what was wrong?
she answers that the table worried her   so strong

and stable at the centre of their daily life...
but if a wind rose, say, or saints turned deaf

if one day food ran out   would it be determined
as a table truly has to be   to carry nothing?

PLEASURES OF THE FEAST

*Poseidon was gone on a visit to the distant Ethiopians, the farthest
outpost of mankind… to accept a sacrifice of bulls and rams, and
there he sat and enjoyed the pleasures of the feast.*
– Homer, The Odyssey

No! think of them as our close cousins
Poseidon as the sea-god lurking in our eyes

come to taste the marrow of the south
and bring a praise song back to Greece…

so let me paint
the pleasures of the feast:

these wine-dark boys who harvest-dance
with three-toed pigeon girls, boys again for hawks

white-robed attendants stood like fountains
gushing icy water onto outstretched hands

fish-nimble servers balancing their trays
of whitest cheese and aromatic just-killed meats

a princess roasting coffee beans
a king who booms his welcome through a horn…

and in the centre, we/Poseidon, holding
one blue hand aboard his chariot

thrust our trident deep into the feast…
don't call it greed   our song is everything we eat

ELEGY FOR A THUNDERSTORM

What is a storm if not weeping?
  and the boy
washing himself in the storm
  with rough hands
and soap   is he not a slim trunk of water
attracting thirsty looks on the track?

rain grieves when our loved-ones
  suffer drought
it fills our ears with sadness
  how can we not weep
when rain weakens
and the storm is bled?

one restless afternoon
  a thunderstorm
like a stampede of buffalos
like a panther hide thrown over the earth
  roaring and hissing
like a colossal road traffic accident

on the muddiest section
  of motorway
between Addis Ababa and the underworld
  when everyone rats
into their holes and the town sags
and starts to break apart

the possibilities for great
   naughtiness
spring up amongst wet children
   even rainbuckets
lick their lips as another thunder crash
unties a row of houses

and the storm looks at itself, amazed
   by its own strength
frightened even, knows full well
   this is too much
water in an old box of drought
too purple this shower

for a folk with such clean noses
a religion washed
   in Nile-water
so the storm looks for a tap
   somewhere up there
in the kitchen clouds

and turns itself off
   to peels
of great bell-drops banging down on roofs
that cause even the roofs
   them-tin-selves
and the boy scrubbing his arms

to beat this elegiac
   drum roll
for the unforgettable thunderstorm
   of their life
since none of us is half as
strong as our desires

WHEN THE BACKYARD WAS A BOY

it liked to hear trees talking   dogs shuffling
hedgehog dozing in an old truck tyre

loved the feet who kicked a ball around in it
chickens pecking in a coop in it

the cook who came out followed by his cooking smells
and told them stories set in Europe and America

where backyards were as big as fields   with apple trees
and toolsheds and an oily garage

but also with a lot of things to groan and be ashamed of
backyards often poor   neglected   hungry

owners being told to look in them   but always better things
to do   busy polishing the smile on their front door

WHEN I WAS TEN, I STARTED WATCHING MEN

Some walk into a sunbeam
and their heads catch fire

some smoke an arm around their friend
or saunter hand in hand with him

others keep their shyness like a torch
inside the pocket of their trousers

unzip themselves against a wall
and whistle as their boiling water flows

many have the necks of swans
that suddenly swing round to look at you

hundreds every day are causing bushfires
to break out   boys' tongues to parch

   be my boy wife!

one calls   but hotly not in words
from the beautiful jet coals of his eyes

THE FIG WASP

There is a way some boys eat a fig
which is like the fig wasp

they point their little tongue and send it
darting through the ostiole

do they lose their wings? lay their eggs
in the place they were born?   perhaps

but when they are inside the fig
they sometimes seem to turn into one

their head fills with sticky red flowers
their cock becomes purple and fleshy

they fall in love with cuts and bruises
anything which shows them

what is happening under the skin
through the ostiole   into the heart of

who they are becoming
how delicious it will be to be ripe

BANANAS

Abebe is fasting
  why?
for Lent or an apostle's day?
Gehad or Nineveh?

he's not in jaunty mood
but still the boy asks
  why?
not *why today?* just *why?*

Abebe's eyes grow
angels
  so my flesh obeys
the will of my immortal soul!

but now the boy's mind too
is wandering
  along
a path of questions

Abebe, can a hungry person fast
or does his soul
  take pity
and give him a banana?

IN GHERALTA

A beautiful rock-church! his mother cries   driving
                                                   over
                                                   a cliff

they live   but see rock-churches   differently
          wary of the spells they cast

the voice that drags you up a mountain just to lurk
          in its little gloom

a church   but has no cross   no tabot   not a single
          prayer stick

and yet   there's something hermit here   that eats you
          from the inside

selfless sleepless   straining   sweating   chipping   chipping
          at your toughest rock

and when you turn to leave   you stop   astonished
          by the view

                              stupendous peaks!

     vast plateaus!

                                        never-ending skies!

and over there   a tiny sunlit village on a hillside

                              could anyone be as blessed?

BECOMING BIG

Suddenly they realise   we will be big!

those big men with their big hands
and broad shoulders
for carrying a globe

they are us!   they are me!

we will look down on fathers and grandfathers
soon the long street will be short   a tall building
                                        not so tall...

the fat man was not fat at all   just full of love

and those figures in the shadows   those thinnesses
high on wooden scaffoldings
who sometimes teeter
minutes
before they fall

why does nobody see them?
they are small
until they hit the ground

but the crater on the pavement is very very big

PRAISE SHOUT FOR A STOMACH

You
who hangs inside me
like a leopard in a thorn acacia tree!

you
greedy for a curried goat
for *iskunfur* and kidneys cooked in wine!

you
always proudly sniffing
always readying a soupdish of digestive juices!

to you
who laughs at bottled waters
sneers at all the wormy devils in raw beef

how dare I wail my banquet of thin songs?
how dare I have no conquering basket of injera?
no optimistic chicken?

MALNOURISHED

Mal
so close to meal

statistics lie
but still today

one in four children, stunted
one in ten, hanging by a thread
one in twenty, dead

I SHAVE MY SOFT HAIR

starting with a verse by Mekonnen Galaacha
singing Geerarsa, the poetry of Oromia

I shave my soft hair
I shave my soft hair
hoping beautiful curly hair will grow

I sing my shrill voice
I sing my shrill voice
hoping a rich smooth voice will grow

I run my small feet
I run my small feet
hoping a pair of marathons will grow

I tug my novice chin
I tug my novice chin
hoping a long wise beard will grow

I read my crinkle books
I read my crinkle books
hoping a brain the size of Addis Ababa University grows

I pat my ropey belly
I pat my ropey belly
hoping a beautiful fat paunch will grow
hoping a beautiful fat paunch will grow

QULUL

after the boasts of Afar warriors

I am Qulul, son of the hot winds
cousin of war and taxes

I am not one who pretends he kills
I am the one who kills

I knocked Harara off his skeleton horse
I knocked his horse down too

I burst Bayleo's swollen belly like a gourd
no food flew out, just air

the man who said he would not run from hardship
the man with silver laces in his sandals

I turned his anus into a tap today
and then I opened it

people ask   *who killed them?* someone answers   *Qulul!*
people say   *Qulul is cruel*   why?   I do not know

last month a Dobi herder offered his last cow
for an abundant girl

but after sixteen days I came back with my spear
and shouted   *she is mine!*

I sucked her perfect cheeks   her bottom fat   I drank the waters
from her body until she turned into a leaf

people say that I am cruel   why?   I do not know
they say I am unnatural   I do not know why

TO A TIN SHACK BEHIND THE LION'S DEN HOTEL

for Biruk

Three people squeeze their lives between
    your narrow shoulders
so open up your wavy door   let morning
    step right in

gift this granny with her pan of coffee beans
    a little sunlight
no-one knows how old she is
    not the small boy

yawning by a nail that holds his satchel
    not his sister
out just now to wash herself   not even you
    ramshackle shack!

but we smell her coffee   taste the montane earth
    in which it grew   and how her little
shuffle of the pan is comforting, familiar...
    its repetition

holds your walls together   keeps your roof
    from lifting in a storm
it confronts time, confuses it   says don't even think
    of buckling in this tawny wind!

HUNGRY, WE

who have no clue
what hunger is

who think that pain
is just a scratch

when we collapse
inside and out

into a hollow
by the gate

because the feelings
got so strong

they got on top of us
and crumpled us

then hunger
slips a pang

into our belly
and we want

SMALL ANGRY FAMINE

Hama does not remember it
nobody remembers it

but he sees people shuffling into Addis
something beaten in their feet

now he starts to hear complaints
half-poems shouted in the streets

and years   years later   when Fekadé
forages around the hills around Wereilu

he finds that people   still can barely
bring themselves to speak about it calmly

but sometimes   standing on one foot
they fish an angry couplet from their throat

አህያ መጣች ፥ ተጭና በለስ
aheya met'ach, tech'na beles

here comes a donkey
loaded with figs

OUTSIDE THE GATES   WITH ABEBE

Friday, early evening

ravishing

ball gown

splashed

with polka dots

gold necklace

silver shoes

all his mother's

fancy dress

breathless

for the party

Monday, noonish

you gypsy curls   you bunny ears   you popgun up a tree

your joy-pink father springs out of his car

HURRAY!!

AFRICA UNITED!!

Buyené smiles (because a smile is close to God)

Buyené who receives the briefcase   puts a whisky soda on the table

LUNCH

gates go quiet   doze like horses standing up

kept in   kept out   dogs agitate

butterflies   in love with the warm air   negotiate

later everything begins   not so you'd notice   blurring

whispers   like someone trying not to wake a tree

Hailu   cotton-dressed   invites all shades of shadow to himself

all the greys of sleep

Tuesday, mid-morning

flamingo boy   one-footed   watching through the gates

the track trots past   discussing life and God   and pissing

there is something he finds pleasing in these metal bars

porous, gentle   like a tug   even lordly horses pause

to study him   drovers' eyebrows curl like question marks

sparrow boys skip close   throw laughbombs at him

shout   *ferenj!*   and giggle   run off   wet their pants

sometimes other words fly out   but words are gates too

not all of them are open to him   anyway, the feeling is

Thursday, 4-ish

dozing in a gap where gates sprout arms and grab the wall…

looks up

two donkey jacks approach and lower

their long penises

in flood they ask

are you Prince Rasselas living on a mountain

in the Happy Valley?

are all your wants catered for but still you long to see

the miseries of the world?

and laugh so hard they bray   and bray so hard they almost burst

Friday, first thing

his eyes go walking   almost far as Ras Mekonnen Bridge…

a fig tree drenched in purple   so the famous lake of purple must be dry…

an old man snoozing in his shawl   mouth open if a fig decides to fall…

a radio off singing to itself   a very pretty woman dancing…

out of nowhere   Abebe screams!   screams!

foot frantic   kicking at the air   a long thick nail sticks out

like a demon   blood dripping on the kitchen steps

Asfaw throws a window wide   Aster   shrieking

                                    flies out of at least three doors

but all the boy can think is

        beautiful!   how beautiful!

Abebe's wounded foot   takes his small breath away

oh! to kiss it

                    he kisses it

Saturday, after breakfast

through one of many windows   (house or car?)

he spies a small girl gawking   through the gates

a King-of-King's-horse-splendid house!

he thinks, surprised   is this really where he lives?

he takes his eyes out   checks them

yes, these gates stand proud!   these windows shine!

everything is gleaming   not just paint

not just the Zephyr   resting in its open garage

if the house was a man   it would be   just back from the barber's!

if it was a feeling   would be   *what could go wrong?*

if it was a boy   be   sucking wine gums all day long…

Sunday, matins

St Matthew's church extended   bread of heaven

pouring out   father singing   feed me til I want no more

my God I'm starved, he says   *hell's bells*, he says under his breath

when Mrs Benedict attacks a descant   when the chaplain

purples about sin   father doodles devils, pitchforks

on his hymnbook   choirboys dipped in boiling oil

little cries like

back home   a goldrush to the dining room

even sunshine here is hungry

    food smells so good on Sundays!

Buyené holds a dish of lamb and roast potatoes, minted peas

Buyené pours the gravy with his other hand

his hand is generous   his smile is definitely godly

Sunday, afternoon

out walking   Abebe and boy   but what is this?

 a mule ripped open by a truck on Yeka Road!

guts spilling from its belly   oh! its head

is smashed   its poor red eyes are popping out

no-one wants to look   but everybody looks

a crowd has grown around it like the rim of a great hole

flies dance   dart   maybe sing

boy tries his hardest to look somewhere else

but soon gives up

                            flinching

thrilled

                                        outside the gates

            with Abebe

አህያ መጣች ፥ ተጭና ችግር
aheya met'ach, tech'na cheger

here comes a donkey
loaded with troubles

TAGESSE'S HUNGER POEMS

All this happened because we did not pray enough
– famine proclamation of Emperor Menelik II, 1890s

I ask for an egg but the Nine Saints say
there is a shortage of hens, even in the sky...

I argue with God over a finger of honey
He who doesn't even have a tummy!

today Ennaté cooked a fasting dish
of pigweed in the shape of a fish

how I long for a barley-cake
to have mercy on my stomach ache!

I begged our cows to praise the Lord
with milk   but they cannot have heard

I begged our fields to praise the Father
with wheat   but they only worship weather

our village formed a committee to talk about the drought
but its members were too thirsty to work anything out

Abbaté is sick and tired of saying
thank-you
thank-you thank-you
thank-you thank-you thank-you
thank-you   thank-you   thank-you   thank-you   thank-you
when he has no reason to thank anyone for anything

ayee! the weekly market in Wereilu
is pointless as a cookpot with no stew

our old ox died this morning
so we chew its skin…
how strong and fat it was before it was thin!

wey! just a bunch of nettles
and no water to boil the kettle

what killed my best friend Yared?
hunger   or the wrath of God?

Yared used to say horse beans are like princes
they ride around in carts and stick up their noses

Yared used to say he'd sell his mother
for a plate of lentils, but his mother
said she'd sell her brother
to make Yared live a minute longer

hungry when I wake up   hungry when I sleep
hungry when I pray for   hungry when I hope
hungry when I go to school   hungry in my head
hungry when I come back home   hungry in my bed

here comes a donkey loaded with dung
our faces look old but our faces are young

I love Saint Mary! whispers my Ennat
no matter I am skinny and She is fat

famine is the price of sin!
our priests are always certain

the Abuna says prayer kills locusts and flies
so we spray it on our crops like pesticide!

hyenas in the hills, romping, feasting
the supply of dead bodies is everlasting

somewhere not far away
a vulture is waiting
for a baby to stop breathing

at the shepherd boy's funeral yesterday
everyone cried and forgot to be hungry

Ennaté saw God today: He is getting thin
because we are too weak to praise Him

a monk with yellow eyes told me a story:
he saw Salvation walk out of the monastery
waving a stick and looking for a bakery

here comes a donkey loaded with almond cakes
just another poem playing tricks

a hungry man from Robit ate his brother's sock
why not his tasty leather hymn-book?

my brother feared the future, so he bought a rope
I'm tying myself to the ankle of hope!

my sister's stomach groaned so loud last night
that Sleep woke up screaming and ran out

who will weep for me, young boy from a poor family?
I am not brave or strong, I cannot grasp the hoe firmly

this morning, Ennaté was so troubled
that she wobbled, stumbled, crumpled
on the floor   she tried so hard
to say something   before she died

a home without a mother
like a cattle farm, no fodder

Abbaté is being eaten by grief
I cannot stay here without my wife!

Abbaté rode away but the reins went loose
the mule saw that his heart was still in the house

slowly

slowly

slowly...... the whisper becomes a shout:
rain is falling on the tongue of the drought!

                    is that God up there in the high branches
                    throwing down figs from the high branches?

                                                    !

berberé has come back, t'eff too, and abish
afrinj is in the market, so is t'ella, so is t'ej

                    oily fingers are here again and colourful breath
                    but nothing can bring back Ennaté from her death

I shouted at famine, although it could not hear
now I will only speak to things with an ear

                    my name is *Tagesse*: *he endured*
                    I am a boy who has hungered

fresh butter is golden, plentiful as mud
so newborn babies will be anointed and fed

        cowherds are singing, shepherd boys are merry
all because of the num-num trees and num-num berries

no thanks to the committee
no thanks to the sky

                        not by begging from strangers
                    not by crying through my fingers

not by trying to be clever
not pretending to be strong...

                            I am not a dried out river!
                            I have only just begun!

                        here comes a donkey loaded with wheat
                    here comes God again, putting on weight

አህያ መጣች ፤ ተጭና ተስፋ
aheya met'ach, tech'na tesfa

here comes a donkey
loaded with hope

LIB

Here is only one small word for mind and heart
so Biruk tells me to *have lib* when crossing Smuts

its wildest spot! six lanes stampeding
just a monosyllable to see us over to the other side

but *lib* being made of air must also trust our fragile body
to deliver it   our nimble feet are *lib's* philosophy

TO THE TEEMING BOOKSHOPS OF ADDIS ABABA

A thirst for knowledge being one
of the most urgent
do you see this brush-stroke racing
along Arat Kilo

       up the length of Wingate

              into Piassa?

if stopped, either by his shirttails   flying!
or a hand on his athlete's shoulder
or his thoughts   also flying...
he would say a rumour reached him

    too loud for day-dreams!

that a new translation of Rimbaud's

    Le Bateau Ivre

is hitting the choppy water of your shelves
although he already owns a tattered copy
in the French

      two more in English

          one of almost holy status

             in Amharic

    Yesekere Merkeb!

to see the same loved, breathing body of the poem
behind the gauze of each re-working
only adds to his excitement   knowledge not in facts

but in the energy of words racing
from language   to language   bookshop   laptop
on their bare feet
                        fitter

                                    leaner

                                                faster
the more they are taken into the thin air
of the mountains

                                            and stretched

THE RED BICYCLE

How does one truly nourish a hungry human soul?
– L.R. Kass

Cocked against a lamppost
by the old Taitu Hotel

> *hop on!*

I say   let's zip around the town
and see what's happening

how lives rub up against each other

shall we take tea at the Pankhursts?
oh, to be British *and* Ethiopian!

Richard says

> *I only know dead poets*

so that animated ghost under a fig tree
must be Tsegaye Gabre-Medhin?

> *yes, he's been reciting*
> *this long poem*
> *for the last ten years…still*
> *only half way through, I think…*

the ghost gets to his feet
and saunters off   so jump back on!
let's bump along this praise-path
to the army hospital

64

                    soon men in hats
and dusty jackets join us children
with their hands held tightly by their mothers
day-off soldiers out of uniform
shall we offer one a lift sideways on my crossbar?

Tsegaye's ghost has gathered a wide river of admirers
other poets stroll with us and twirl their pens

Kebede Mikail still smokes a cigarette he lit
it must be thirty years ago

Zewdu counts his syllables and Mekdes tugs
a chicken from her latest book

at last, a café where I fling myself
against the jacaranda that I know so well

        a hundred macchiatos, please!

Tsegaye still reciting   don't forget
we come from every corner of Ethiopia
in our minstrel buses   rhythm taxis

on our centuries of leather feet

we learn to rub together in Amharic
while our eighty other languages sit quietly at home...

now Mulu opens her pink purse to buy a millefeuille
        oozing custard cream!

first she offers half to Tsegaye who studies it
intently   an image of delight?   a metaphor?

he finishes   but still the cake is sitting there
            miraculous
and Mulu too is toying with her half   not eating it

my handlebars grow twitchy   time to go
but wait! a scruffy boy is scampering towards us

        I'm hungry like a crocodile!

he cries   Mulu shakes her cake-fork   cries back

        child, you are a poem I have longed to write!

her eyes so dark before   light up   her braids
fizz like a battery even Tsegaye dims a little
Kebede's cigarette goes out   pens clatter to the ground
as Mulu slowly starts to feed a slice of millefeuille
into the boy's mouth
                    bountifully as a queen

THREE BUSHTI GO TO THE MERCATO

for Beki & Mike

A trio of cursed boys
two short, one tall   hair in corkscrews
so the air must feel it

dawdle in Tomoca
sipping three lion cups of coffee
from Harar

before they sally out again
freely but together   small fleet of lake-dhows
into the souks

sailing by the wind
of their smiles   by the elegance of their fingers
that praise a belt just touching it

and one stallholder they call *Gash*é
(meaning *My Shield*   to show affection for the older man
who treats them lightly but with dignity)

halloos his welcome
(as you would too   don't you thirst for tolerance?   a little boat
of colour on the lake of everyday…?)

shouting
>   *my fellow citizens!*
>   *my brave zegoch!*

and all his merchandise
of skimpy T-shirts   wild netalas   liberated jeans
get up on their feet   and ᎪᎪᎪᎪ....!   and sing

UNCLE! TAKE ME TO A BETTER PLACE

Streetlamps simmer
railings burn with countryboys

an old man stops and smiles
but where is that? he says

how could a young man
be more beautiful than you?

where could an old man smile
like this and still have teeth?

THE SHOP ON MY CHEST

suk bedereté

A shelf of chewing gums and bubble gums and tissues
on a thong around his neck
his prow in heavy crowds until light fades
and still he goes on calling

Orion Banana!

Kleenex!

in the half-dark spaces under soapberry trees
where soft words linger with a cigarette
and sometimes you can hear a coin
drop into the soukboy's unfathomable pocket

TO A WEYALA/MINIBUS CONDUCTOR

You littlemouth who flourishes the door
    and barks *Bolé! Bolé!*
you pickupquick
you dropoffsafe
you tuttertongue and crammer of the empty seat
you fingerfox of notes and coins
you griptoe swivelhead
you dieselgulpy littleshirt
you pencilneck
you wooden cross
you deacon of the minibus, bowing to the altar of your task
    believing in it absolutely
you furrowbrow and grindesert
you eyecaptain
you brave commanding
you swaggerlad who takes so many where they want to go
take me

FOR THE SERVAL CATS

whose skins are being touted
through car windows   for your flat

heads and pointy ears beyond hearing
for your shoe-lace legs unravelling

over the knees of potential buyers
for your nails on their thighs

and their fingers in your pelt
for the life-force that you left

running about
in the echo of the shot

and for you too, brothers of these skins
who outwit the hunters' guns

with strings of such mischievous hops
over grass-tickled rocks

that Ethiopians say the little hyraxes and hares
you pounce on   sing your praise

NEVER A BAD WORD ABOUT HYENAS!

after Edwin Morgan's Hyena and an old Ethiopian superstition

All day I chased you in my dream
now you are sleeping in a room you think is safe
but it is not safe   it has an unlocked window
anything you say inside this room   I will hear
even if you only think it   I will hear

I live on Mount Entoto but I come down
into the city to eat   you are one of the lions
who do my killing for me   you are kind
I rip open the flanks of your rubbish bins and feast
do not ask me to be quiet   I am in your head

at three o'clock there is no one but the moon
and me in your garden   I have greased
my spots to slip the gates   now I pad
over the rough grass towards your window
do not be afraid   you are expecting me

you never said anything bad about hyenas
but on the other hand   you said nothing good
you will not feel pain   only a mild regret
to have missed the hunger you saw in others
to be not quite as safe on this earth as you thought

THE YOUNG MEN SAY

We live like chickens   the young men say
just eating and sleeping

we're explosive   the young men say   as soon as we're not boys
you throw us out into the street and close your ears

our hope is cut   the young men say   there is no proper work for us
so we chew khat and watch a film all afternoon

there is some wash-up work in cafeterias   the young men say
but friends will drop their heads and leave us to our shame

Afeworq   the young men say   with his degree in maths and logic
now a bicycle repairer   finding ways to do the jobs that no-one has a tool for

his work is not so bad   but it is on the street   the young men say
so Afeworq is always naked to the gaze and judgement of the world

Getnet is a barber in a shop   *he* is not dirtied by gazes
good!   the young men say   but still he has to touch our hair

WHEN BERBERÉ ATTACKS

it kicks the man out of his car and dumps him
burning, groaning, shitting on the ground...
it knows he smells Abebe in its heat
his coloured tongue   the promise of...
for fifty years they have been friends
(Abebe dying changes nothing)
and berberé has kept its jealousy
just under boiling point   not now!
the emergency clinic is in front of him
but berberé will not allow the man to stand
he must be carried like a baby shivering
and mewling   laid out on a bed like on a skillet
frying in the sweat he makes   chilli oil
could not be hotter or more terrible
berberé laughs   and when the stomach lining
and the throat can scream no louder
it decides to take its sword to Abebe
to cut Abebe down and throw him into places
where all feelings wither   optimism dies
and the simple way a child loves is not brooked
because it has no syrup   no result
there is no wedding bell for it   no hospital
but if the man survives   he knows he will
wake up to find that berberé is dead
and Abebe still standing on a sunny street

THREE PICKPOCKETS

Three pickpockets push and pull him across the road
they are furious with him, try to get into his pockets
but his pockets will not cooperate   his pockets press
their lips firm shut and say we're not saying a word
but eventually they concede ok, take his wallet if you must
there's not much in it   he will have to ring a few numbers
to stop his credit cards going on sprees   he will re-apply
for a driving licence but that's not the end of the world, is it?

    and I can see you are very hungry...

that's the man talking now, he can see it in the way their eyes
refuse to look at him, being red and full of glue   even they
know this is not them, not really their hands gripping his arms
their fingers attacking his pockets, as God is their witness
and if Satan were not at work tonight at the Atlas Crossroads
all bellies would bulge!   all pockets leak on principle!
each arrogant wad of notes fall under a ton of shame!
all roads would flood with coins so flush that people's hands
fill up just by opening   and no man ever have to wipe
the thieving off his fingers or dig the fluffy greed out of his pocket

TRUTH DOG

Poor thing, squinty
patchy, limpy
tails me all the way to Siddist Kilo
sits under my table in the café
by the University
tells the waiter bring a bowl of water
barks that he will share my food

look, neither of us is fond of fleas
    or any good with hunger
both of us believe a dog may love the dog he chooses
howling costs even the howler his own bodyweight in sleep
but if you dare neglect me one more time, old man
I will slink off to a corner of this cruel city
and you will never forgive yourself

ABEL MIGRATING

My brave young friend migrating

north along the Blue Nile pedalling

almost to heaven climbing, then like a kite down from the peaks

    free-wheeling

in Metemma through greasy fingers slipping, on a Sahara-lorry

    jumping, scrambling

in your dust-scarf backwards facing, at night for tins and bottles digging

    hardly sleeping , never loving

finally in Tripoli arriving, hardmen meeting, all your wealth disposing

no power enjoying but salt air breathing, dangers scorning, gangplank striding

into the future pushing, with your brothers the great gamble taking

fulfilling what you dreamed

THE DAY THEY MURDERED ASSEFA MARU

was the day of the last straw   the bitterest pill
      the day I decided to become a refugee
the day I phoned my sister but what was there to say?

the day I thought about the fiery speech Assefa Maru made
      to the Union of Teachers in Addis Ababa   the day
I buried my Ethiopian passport under a foot of London clay

the same day Assefa Maru was walking to his office
      near the Good Shepherd NGO   and a Toyota
stopped suddenly in front of him   blocking his peaceful way

and an Opel with a siren raced up the street and a policeman
      in the back seat fired a burst of pistol shots
before Assefa Maru could cry out   before he could pray

the day that Assefa Maru died   the first of many days
      when I shouted   *Thank you, God, for saving me!*
and whispered all along the way to the newspaper shop

thank you Britain for allowing me to stay
      and people said I must become a British citizen
forget your fiery friend, Tamrat   you are a teacher of today!

but it was also the evening of the day when I drove that thought away
      when something quiet, almost clay, inside me
started dreaming of the day I would go out into my garden

and dig it up again, my country   singing *Oh yes, this is the day!*

IN THE LION GARDENS

Old men sitting by the apple trees
            can you hear me?
I am an old man too   we've shrunk inside our shirts
our coffees are so strong they may outlive us

I look for Tagesse   *who's he?*   a boy
            who I imagined in the famine
when we both were boys   Tagesse shouting at it   scraping by
in it   grieving and enduring   like the meaning of his name

he must be getting on   an old imagined man
            no, I did not send him
to another famine or the Eritrean war   I did not forcibly
resettle him in Illubabor   I could not write more suffering

            *wendim*é!

says Tagesse and rises from a bench of smiles
            because he made it through
his being here is blessed!   he comes towards me   autumn eyes
and winter hair   a courteous old man of Ethiopia

but do I clap him on the back when I had food
            and he did not?   his life and mine
his acre of the mountains   worlds apart   Tagesse, sit with me
beside the cages   old lions have such splendid manes!

tell me your story from the start
            not its surrendered facts
but every feeling just as you remember it
we'll sit here for a month, a year   the apple trees won't mind

until my ears are bleeding and my heart has stopped…
　　　　my joy in boyhood filled
a thousand fizzy bottles   kicked at sadness like a mule
but now I'm liverish, light-headed   old stomach trying to digest

the plate of misery it missed   just as your happiness
　　　　will always be half-starved
by wants and horrors which I heaped upon you years ago

　　　　open your eyes!

you shout at me, but not unkind   so I stand up
and look   at you, at me   and feel that I am falling

CHICKEN IS THE SAFEST THING

Madiba was being freed that day

ayeee! what a big day!

he would stay the night at Bishopscourt
and his first meal should be tasty and filling

so Lillian Ngoboza chose a comforting recipe
of Mrs Tutu's floured chicken breasts with spices

browned and simmered them
until they were lovely

really lovely!

the people were so hungry to greet him
that he needed a long time to reach the house

at last he came and everyone sat down
and Lillian served the curried chicken with a salad

afterwards he visited the kitchen to thank her
it was his first meal of freedom after many years

a meal like that must not disappoint, he said
it must be warm and honest   it must say

welcome back to your life!

the sort of food that fills a belly with determination
throws the prison door wide open in your head

PRAYER TO A SAINT OF TWO RELIGIONS

Prayer rusts! says Alemu
whose father has a sickness of the heart
and needs a lot of help from heaven

so Alemu takes words like
   mercy   penitence
and oils them in his mouth

only when they shine like trumpets
does he blast his prayer
through St Gabriel's wings

to lift his angel high into the sky
above the perfect circle of the village church
the simple white square of the masjid

A SONG: YEHAGERÉ SHETA

Tilahun is hungry
for *The Smell of my Country*

the injera his mother made
a scented fig tree in the yard

his voice goes up and up
and teeters on his own dry lip

above ethnicities
and rivalries

all the niggles
and the quibbles

into the warm bone
of his microphone

ABOUT THE COWS AT LAKE LANGANO

Who better than a cook's son to observe the hunger
of others?   to stand quite close   by a tree or a tent flap

with his butterfly grin   and one or two tunes
playing from the radio of his mouth and lungs

seeing the English father's hands' uneasiness
but his children's fingers frolicking in injera and stew

the boy who glances back at him   delighted   freckled
sauces dripping even from his elbows   cheeks on fire

and cowherds who have driven cattle to the lake to drink
but refuse the cook's kind offer of some food and a drink

because they are quiet   sunk in their old ways
shy of any variation   taste or presentation

for what that might imply about the world   their place in it
better not to look around   not lordly bellies   but full enough

the cattle in milk   in good blood too to mix with the milk
if you nick their necks   carefully   gently

yes, this Abebe knows because he has observed it
and tells the boy how the red milk tasted flowery and sweet

how the cow stared into his eyes as he drank from a gourd
and how the cowherd stood there   watching

AMHARIC GLOSSARY

ሰሰሰሰ	elelelel…., approximating the sound of ululation
abbat	father (abbaté, my father)
abish	fenugreek
Abuna	head of the Ethiopian Orthodox church
afrinj	powdered red pepper seeds
berberé	a fiery powder made from red chilies, garlic, ginger, rue seeds, sacred basil, cloves, cinnamon, cardamom and bishop's weed… it provides the kick in most Ethiopian dishes!
bushti	a common pejorative for gay
ennat	mother (ennaté, my mother)
ferenj	foreigner (probably derived from "French")
injera	the staple sourdough pancake of Ethiopia, made from t'eff, a tiny but highly nutritious grain grown in the highlands
iskunfur	tripe stuffed with onions, ginger and rice
khat	a stimulant, people chew the leaves and hold them in their cheek
mesob	the raised basket on which injera and stews/sauces are placed
netala	a shawl made of cotton gauze, mostly white with a brilliantly patterned and coloured stripe around the edge
t'ella	mild aromatic beer made with woody hops and roasted barley
t'ej	honey wine

t'ibs	strips of beef fried with spiced butter, onions, garlic and berberé
wendim	brother (wendimé, my brother)
wey!	woe, sorrow
wot	a meat, chicken or fish stew normally made with berberé
zega/zegoch	citizen(s)
zilbo	a stew made with dried beef, onions, fenugreek and powdered peas

NOTES

Aheya met'ach, tech'na.../ Here comes a donkey loaded with...
Many Ethiopian folk poems start with this phrase, although
its meaning is usually unconnected with the rest: it is there
simply to set up the rhythm and rhyme of the poem. But the
ubiquitous donkey – what he carries and how much, also how
well-fed he is himself – is still a bellwether for the health and
happiness of the rural economy.

Ras Gugsa's kindness
Ras means *head* or *self* in Amharic, but is also a title equivalent
to duke. Ras Gugsa was the fourth husband of Empress
Zewditu, and a rival of Haile Selassie for the succession. He
was killed at the Battle of Anchem in 1930. I am indebted for
the details here to Kessis Kefyalew Merahi's book *The meaning
of Quine: The River of Life* (Addis Ababa, 2006). But that
Gugsa handed out trays of food on the battlefield is a fiction
of mine, though not out of character perhaps.

When the backyard was a boy
Prompted by something James Baldwin said in an interview
with Studs Terkel in 1961: 'White people in New York talk
about Alabama as though they had no Harlem. To ignore
what is happening in their own backyards is a great device on
the part of white people.' (*James Baldwin, the Last Interview
and Other Conversations,* Melville House, 2014)

When I was ten, I started watching men
The title quotation is adapted from an interview with a young Kikuyu resident of Nairobi in *Boy-Wives and Female-Husbands: Studies in African Homosexualities* edited by Stephen O. Murray and Will Roscoe (Palgrave Macmillan, 1998).

Qulul
After *War Chants in Praise of Ancient Afar Heroes, collected by George C Savard*, published in the Journal of Ethiopian Studies (edited by Richard Pankhurst). In putting some of the language of these warrior boasts into the mouth of Qulul (Famine), I am following a tradition in Ethiopian poetry, where the cause of human distress eg jigger fleas or disease or famine, is given a voice to boast and mock, even to demand pity from the people it is hurting.

Outside the gates   with Abebe
Africa United: the Organisation of African Unity (now the African Union) was inaugurated in Addis Ababa in May, 1963. The donkeys' quotation is from Samuel Johnson's 1759 tale about the pursuit of happiness, *The History of Rasselas, Prince of Abissinia.*

Tagesse's hunger poems
These couplets were written to honour, by imitating, Ethiopian oral famine poems, like those in Fekade Azeze's *Unheard Voices: Drought, Famine and God in Ethiopian Oral Poetry (Addis Ababa University Press, 1998),* which date from famines in the 1960s, 70s and 80s. Because of their regular metre, full rhymes, and often sardonic tone, it is easy to underestimate the suffering that lies behind this poetry. The poets rarely describe their pain, but they complain about everything and everyone, particularly God, and it is this indignation and defiance I admire so much and wanted to try and get inside, by imagining a boy about my

own age at the time experiencing the famine of the mid 1960s which killed an estimated 50,000 people. Incidentally, I do not want to give the impression that Ethiopia is still a land of famine: the population has risen from around 25 to over 100 million and there is still much poverty and hunger, even some deaths (under-reported no doubt), but mechanisms have been put in place over the past 30 years to forewarn and prevent food shortages becoming catastrophic. A good account of this is given in Alex de Waal's *Mass Starvation: The History and Future of Famine* (Polity Press, 2018).

Three bushti go to the Mercato
Bushti is a common Amharic pejorative for gay, derivation unknown. Mercato is the vast open market in the west of Addis Ababa. Tomoca is a popular coffeeshop in the Piassa district, with a huge painting of a lion roaring over its coffee machines. Zega (plural zegoch), meaning citizen, is what gay Ethiopians often call each other, ironically, since they have no rights at all, except in the republic of their imagination.

The young men say
Based on Daniel Mains' study of the complex forces behind high rates of youth unemployment in Ethiopia, *Hope is Cut* (in the 'Global Youth' series published by Temple University Press). The Amharic for 'hopeless' is 'tesfa qoretwa', literally 'hope is cut', like a delicate thread between present and future. Young men are often referred to as 'fendata', meaning explosive. The name Afeworq means mouth of gold and Getnet means lordship.

Abel migrating
at night for tins and bottles digging: in order not to have to carry too many supplies across the Sahara on their over-loaded trucks, people traffickers routinely bury tins of food

and bottles of water at certain points which their clients then
dig up during stops.

Chicken is the safest thing

After Anna Trapido's book *Hunger for Freedom*, the story of
food in the life of Nelson Mandela, whose clan name was
Madiba.

A song: Yehagere sheta

Tilahun Gessesse (1940-2009) shot to fame as a young singer
in the late 1950s and his music is still adored throughout
Ethiopia. You can hear the 1970 recording of him singing this
wonderful wailing song on *Ethiopiques 17*, or on YouTube,
accompanied by the Imperial Bodyguard Band.

About the cows at Lake Langano

Drinking their cows' blood is a practice of the Suri people of
south-west Ethiopia, nowhere near Lake Langano. The boy is
a bit confused.

ACKNOWLEDGEMENTS

I would like to thank the editors of the following publications where some of the poems or earlier versions of them first appeared: *London Grip*, *Magma*, *Poetry Wales*, *PN Review*, *The North*, *The Rialto*, *A Boxful of Ideas* (ed. John Dixon & Jeffrey Doorn, Paradise Press 2016).

The day they murdered Assefa Maru was a runner-up in the Troubadour International Poetry Competition, 2014.

Never a bad word about hyenas! was commissioned by the National Poetry Library and the Edwin Morgan Trust for the Edwin Morgan centenary celebrations, 2020

Thanks to Karen McCarthy Woolf and Moniza Alvi for their wonderful insights and encouragement; to my partner Isao for allowing me to use his lovely painting on the cover, also for helping me see the poems more clearly than I could myself and therefore how to improve them; to Jane Duran, Robert Seatter and all my friends in the Thursday Group who helped spark and mould many of the poems; to Zerihun, Yemisrach and Anania Tassew, also Gedilu Dejene, Melkam Desta and Martha Hardy for looking after me so well in Addis Ababa; lastly to Michael Schmidt for helping to edit some of the poems, and to Alemu Tebeje and Hama Tuma for their enduring friendship and advice on all things Ethiopian.